A little b

Mers

Personal memories inspired by The Francis Frith Collection®

THE FRANCIS FRITH COLLECTION

www.francisfrith.com

Based on a book first published in the United Kingdom in 2013 by The Francis Frith Collection®

This edition published exclusively for Bradwell Books in 2013
For trade enquiries see: www.bradwellbooks.com or tel: 0800 834 920
ISBN 978-1-84589-727-7

British Library Cataloguing in Publication Data

A Little Book of Merseyside Memories
Personal Memories inspired by the Francis Frith Collection

The Francis Frith Collection
6 Oakley Business Park,
Wylye Road, Dinton,
Wiltshire SP3 5EU
Tel: +44 (0) 1722 716 376
Email: info@francisfrith.co.uk
www.francisfrith.com

Printed and bound in Malaysia
Contains material sourced from responsibly managed forests

Front Cover: Southport, Peter Pan's Playground c1955 S160047p
Frontispiece: Liverpool, The Mersey Tunnel from the Wellington Column c1960 L60032

The colour-tinting is for illustrative purposes only, and is not intended to be historically accurate

A little book of Memories – A Dedication

This book has been compiled from a selection of the thousands of personal memories added by visitors to the Frith website and could not have happened without these contributions. We are very grateful to everyone who has taken the time to share their memories in this way. This book is dedicated to everyone who has taken the time to participate in the Frith Memories project.

It is comforting to find so many stories full of human warmth which bring back happy memories of "the good old days". We hope that everyone reading this book will find stories that amuse and fascinate whilst at the same time be reminded of why we feel affection for Britain and what makes us all British.

Francis Frith always expressed the wish that his photographs be made available to as wide an audience as possible and so it is particularly pleasing to me that by creating the Frith web site we have been able to make this nationally important photographic record of Britain available to a worldwide audience. Now, by providing the Share Your Memories feature on the website we are delighted to provide an opportunity for members of the public to record their own stories and to see them published (both on the website and in this book), ensuring that they are shared and not lost or forgotten.

We hope that you too will be motivated to visit our website and add your own memories to this growing treasure trove – helping us to make it an even more comprehensive record of the changes that have taken place in Britain in the last 100 years and a resource that will be valued by generations to come.

John M Buck
Managing Director
www.francisfrith.com

"Got any gum, chum?"

I grew up in Raeburn Avenue in Eastham, being nearly five when the Second World War started. People in our avenue lined their windows with lace curtains stuck on with flour and water glue to protect the glass if we should be bombed. A bomb did indeed land in a field a couple of hundred yards away, blowing most of our windows in, and I remember seeing my brother, only a few months old, with the lace curtained window draped across his cot, but thanks to the curtain he was unharmed. A house at the far end of the road got a direct hit from a bomb, which did not explode, but still demolished the house. We got a big lump of shrapnel through our roof which landed on my aunt's bed, but luckily she wasn't in it at the time. When the air-raid sirens went off at night we all had to go across the road and through the garden of a neighbour (Mr Reid, the local air-raid warden) to a gap in the railings which opened out onto Heygarth Road Primary School playing field, where earthen covered air-raid shelters had been built. There we would stay until the 'all clear' siren went. We children used to go out every morning after raids, picking up pieces of shrapnel. Later in the war I remember what seemed to be thousands of American Forces' trucks parked all over the place. A common phrase at the time from us kids to the American servicemen was: "Got any gum, chum?"

Frank Davies

A wartime childhood in Port Sunlight

The photographs of Port Sunlight on the Frith website brought back so many memories that are still as clear as day to me. I first came to live in the village with an aunt and uncle in 1939, so of course the war years were quite prevalent in my experience. I lived at 72 Greendale Road. Wartime air-raids saw us going into the basement of the Lyceum for safety, and in one air-raid the original Mac Fisheries shop was hit by a parachuted landmine and demolished, and much damage was done to houses in our area. The nearby bridge and the Dell was a great area for playing. In winter we children used to sledge almost the full length of it, I don't suppose that would be allowed nowadays, and we'd also bombard the factory girls with snowballs when they turned out – great fun!

Eveline Flint (née Peers)

Port Sunlight, Dell Bridge and the Lyceum c1955 P188036

Definitely not "one of ours"!

We lived in Mill Street in the Dingle area of Liverpool during the war and one night in 1942 our mother took me and my sister to the Mayfair cinema. We saw the picture and as it was ending the air-raid sirens went. The manager said we could stay at the cinema until the 'all clear' sounded, but Mum was worried that Dad would be looking for us, so we started to venture home. We were walking along Aigburth Road when we saw this plane coming down low. Mum said "Don't worry, I think its one of ours". She had no sooner said those words than the pilot of the plane started to machine-gun both sides of the road. Luckily for us we managed to get into an air-raid shelter where Dad found us. I don't think many of our generation nowadays would want to go through anything like that again today.
Ruth Strong

We never got to see the end of our Saturday morning serial!

I lived in Wallasey as a child during the war. We children used to go the Saturday morning pictures at the old Coliseum picture theatre, which was bombed in the war and later rebuilt as the Phoenix. The Saturday morning serial which was showing in weekly instalments before the picture theatre got bombed was 'The Thunder Riders' chapter 2 of the 12-part Gene Autry serial 'The Phantom Empire', and we never got to see the end! But I was in London for some time in the 1950s and a Tatler News Theatre was showing the entire serial, so I sat through the whole lot.   *Bill Howard*

Sheltering in the cellars of the Halfway House Hotel at Birkenhead

When I was very small during the war my family lived at number 295 Woodchurch Road (now demolished) in Birkenhead, next door to the Halfway House Hotel (which is still there), seen in this photograph at the junction with Storeton Road. I still have vivid memories of being taken into its cellars from the age of about 3 to 4 during frequent air-raids around 1941, surrounded by many neighbours, drinking lots of tea, together with the hotel's landlord and landlady, the Murches.

> "Surrounded by many neighbours, drinking lots of tea."

Mike Dennis

Birkenhead, Storeton Road and the Halfway House Hotel 1954 B399007

The war years at Litherland

During the Second World War I lived in Beach Road in Litherland, near Bootle, in a flat on the premises of Lewis's factory where my father was the manager. The factory usually made men's clothing for the Lewis's stores but during the war it made army uniforms. It was very close to the docks and was heavily raided and my parents, along with others, walked the grounds and roof during air-raids to put out incendiary bombs. There was a great deal of poverty near the Lewis's factory at the time and every Christmas morning the factory canteen was open to neighbouring children to come for 'The Robins breakfast' where they were all given a hearty meal, a box of food to take home for their family and a present from Santa Claus.

Joan Rothwell (née Beesley)

We felt like refugees...

Our family lived in Palmerston Drive at Litherland during the war. One of my most vivid memories of that time was when people living in the whole street had to be evacuated during the bombing because of the threat caused by the fire at the nearby Bryant & May matchworks. We walked by foot during the night over the lift bridge into the safety of the countryside, and felt like refugees.

Reg Nicholson

When the war ended...

My family arrived in Seaforth late in 1939 after we were shipped back from Gibraltar where my father was stationed with the King's Regiment. We lived in Holly Grove. In the early part of the Second World War my sister Maureen and I, along with hundreds of other kids, were evacuated to Radnorshire in Wales, but there were still air-raids going on when we returned to our home in Seaforth and we spent many a night in the communal air-raid shelter in the street or down in the coal cellar of our house. Areas of Elm Road and Gladstone Road were destroyed, as was the part of Church Road next to the RC church. Ewart Road and many other streets were also badly damaged. Boys being boys, we had plenty of places to play in, even though we were always being told to stay out of the bombed sites. Then the Americans arrived during the war and were stationed at Seaforth Barracks. When the war ended we had huge street parties to celebrate. To this day I am still surprised as to where all the lovely cakes, sweets and so on for the parties came from, as wartime rationing was very severe.

> "We spent many a night in the communal air-raid shelter in the street or down in the coal cellar of our house."

Charles Hegarty

Collecting the sailors' cigarette packets

I lived at Seaforth as a youngster and teenager in the 1940s and 50s. I remember there was a huge fire in one of the nearby docks one year, I think it was full of rubber, and then some time after that the 'Empress of Canada' (the second ship of that name) caught fire and turned on its side in the Gladstone Dock on 25th January 1953. I can still remember the flames and the heat. Seaforth isn't the same now though – new docks, Elm Road blocked off from Seaforth Road, the new Princess Road, and worst of all, the overhead railway has gone – gosh, the fun we used to have on that! When I was young we could walk into the docks and just about board any ship that was moored there and scrounge a meal off the cooks in the galleys. We would also pick up match and cigarette packets to collect, which had been dropped by the sailors off the boats – they came from all over the world.

Charles Hegarty

Eastham, Eastham Dock c1965   E9504

Excavating Eastham Dock...

I lived in Eastham in the late 1940s and early 1950s at Carlett Park (in the old army camp) during the digging of the dock (opposite). I had a lot of fun riding on the machinery when they were doing it.
William McCully

My dad worked at Birkenhead docks

My dad, Billy Sinnett, worked on the docks at Birkenhead for years when we were small. All the dockers had a nickname, my dad's was 'Crazy Horse' or 'Chief'. I remember him coming home from work carrying a 'docker's hook' as they called it and he hung it up in the cupboard under the stairs.   *Valerie Longmoor*

A docker's hook was a curved steel 'S' hook with a wooden handle that was used by dockers to impale items such as sacks and bales and make them easier to pick up and carry.

Birkenhead, The Docks 1967   B399038

Helping a well-known comedian

I lived at 97 Rudyard Road, Knotty Ash when I was young. Being brought up in Knotty Ash I lived quite close to Liverpool's famous comedian, Ken Dodd. In those early days of his career, in the late 1940s and early 50s, Ken worked as a comedy performer at night and in the day he had a large van and used to go around the area selling pots and pans and other household items. I used to go round knocking on

> "The last time I spoke to you, you were sending me up garden paths knocking on doors."

doors to help him sell the wares. Many years later, around the year 2001, I was at a private show in nearby Prescot in a hotel where Ken was performing. When the show was over I waited for Ken to come back into the room for photographs. I said to him "The last time I spoke to you, you were sending me up garden paths knocking on doors". Immediately he recognised me and replied "Do you remember Alan Shields who was one of our 'gang'?", and then went off with quite a long funny story about Alan. I was amazed at his memory, to remember an event which happened in the 1940s and which he could so easily bring to mind. Ken had an uncle called 'Little Bill', he was only about three foot six inches high, and I am pretty sure that's where Ken got the idea of the 'diddy folk' from.

Gordon Smith

Living in St Helens

From 1964 I used to walk past this church every day on my way to and from Central Modern School in St Helens. There used to be a joke shop opposite, where we bought stink bombs and others tricks. I also remember there used to be a museum in the Victoria Park at St Helens with a huge stuffed tiger, the first time I ever saw it I nearly jumped out of my skin with fright. What a great park it was before they removed the boundary wall. I used to go stickleback fishing there with a worm on a piece of thread and catching newts, those were great days as a kid living in St Helens. I'm now in my sixties...where did the time go? I can remember it as if it was yesterday, even lying down to watch the fish...

John Hayes

St Helens, The Parish Church c1965 S415031

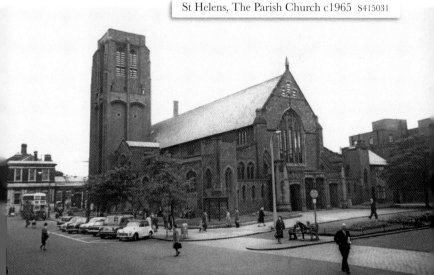

Fishing at the Ram Pit reservoir at Haydock (nicknamed the Cat Pit)

I'm now in my seventies, but I remember lots of things about my younger days living in Haydock in the 1940s and 50s. I used to go fishing in the Ram Pit reservoir, it was behind the shops near the Ram's Head pub. Jack Case had a big yard opposite the Ram's Head that was full of military vehicles after the war, right up to the wooden head gear of the Ram Pit. There was even the body of a glider up there, like the ones they used at Arnhem, the vehicles went right down to the water and we could fish off the backs of them. It was great before they built the council estate off Peel Road. We'd play in the fields where the estate is now, there was a hill where Peel Hall once stood and the remains of a moat. One hundred yards either side of Church Road and you would be in fields.   *Eric Bond*

The games we played at Haydock

It's sad to see all the games we played as kids at Haydock in the past are no longer around – hopscotch, he rolly, hide and seek, tic, the skipping rope, piggy, hig im jig, throw out can, cigarette cards, marbles, all healthy outdoor activities. Just writing about these games on my memory on the Frith website brought back many happy memories, I hope it triggers the same effect on older readers, although I do understand you would need to be getting on a bit to remember these games!   *Kenneth Ashton*

Receiving my certificate

I attended a presentation at St George's Hall in Liverpool as a youngster in 1959, where I received a beautiful certificate in recognition of an essay I had written. I have no idea what I wrote about but since the RSPCA awarded the certificate, I assume it must have been about animals. As a very shy, not-at-all-confident child, I remember nervously waiting and waiting for the moment to come when I had to go on stage for my presentation. At last, I climbed the few stairs alongside the stage and as I stepped forward onto the old wooden stage I immediately tripped and went sprawling at the feet of the adults seated there. I lived to tell the tale but didn't think I ever would!

Lynne McCarrick

Liverpool, St George's Hall c1881 7813

Film shows with the Auntie Gladys club

I was born in St Catherine's Hospital at Tranmere in 1943 and spent the next 22 years living right across the street from it until I emigrated to Canada in 1965. I remember my mother, my sister and I walking along Derby Road with the empty pram to pick up a bag of coal (in the days of rationing)! The corner shop was Morris's just at the bottom of the hill near North Road – we used to go there for a pound of broken biscuits and a little bag of Dolly Mixtures. On Saturday morning we went to the film shows with the Auntie Gladys club from the Birkenhead News – singing to the bouncing ball at the Plaza cinema and watching Cowboy movies at the Regent Cinema on Church Road.

Angela Rickett (née Kavanagh)

Saturdays at 'the Ranch' at Huyton

I was born in 1947, and when I was a child at Huyton we loved going to 'the flicks' at the Mayfair cinema on a Saturday morning. We got our sweets in the shop opposite the cinema before going in. It was always a 'Cowboys and Indians' film, that's why we called the cinema 'the Ranch'. Sometimes the film would snap – well, it actually snapped a lot, and when it did we kids would all bang our feet. It was great fun, you could hear the noise outside, but I don't remember anybody getting thrown out. My friend was posh and her mum paid for us to go upstairs as a treat, but it was better to sit downstairs with the rest of the gang. *Carol May (née Bott)*

Growing up in Woolton

I grew up in the Woolton district of Liverpool, in a house opposite the English Rose pub (at the corner of Mackets Lane and Halewood Drive) in Woolton and went to the primary school in Out Lane. We children spent our summer days playing in the orchard by Watergate Lane, in the Quarry Street and School Lane swing parks, and at Woolton Woods and Camphill. We learned to swim at the tiny Woolton Baths, and after swimming at the baths we could buy chips from the village chippie and a carton of milk from the milk machine at Salisbury farm dairy on the top of Kings Drive. On Saturdays we went to the small cinema in Woolton for the matinee, and galloped home down Out Lane slapping our sides to encourage our imaginary horses, or tying our coats around our necks superhero style.

Lynda Barlow

Reading me the riot act

When I was young and living at Seaforth in the 1940s we used to pay a halfpenny for a bottle of milk at school, but some of us did not like milk so we'd use the money instead to buy a halfpenny barm cake from the bakery on Seaforth Road. My mother found out about my deviousness and dragged me down to the police station just past the old Palladium cinema, where I was promptly marched into a cell and had the riot act read to me by 'old Sam', our local bobby. I took a great liking for milk after that little adventure!

Charles Hegarty

The things I did when I was young!

This memory is from 1968, when my nanna and grandad (Charlie and Winnie Davies) used to write their bets out on a piece of paper and I'd run from their house in Acacia Grove in Seacombe to Alf Spearing's bookie's on Wheatland Lane to put them on for them. My grandad worked for Land and Marine Dredging Co. I used to wait on the step of number 10 Acacia Grove for him to come home from work and get money off him so I could go to the Great Float pub and get his bottles of Guinness from the hatch inside, which was the 'offy' of the pub. I had to stand on a crate so I could knock on the door, I was only 11. The money I got was quickly spent on the penny tray in Heinz's sweet shop on New Street – I didn't go to Giles's shop that was opposite, as she shouted at me and my friends for playing football in the street. Thinking back, you can see her point now, we did smash her shop window!

Tony Williams

Rolling snowballs down the hill

I spent my younger years living on Crossender Road in Crosby in the 1950s. In the winter we had hills nearby, adjacent to the Southport to Liverpool railway line. We used to roll little snowballs down the hills until they achieved a massive girth of a metre. Sometimes they would get out of control and smash into someone's fence or greenhouse – of course we kids were nowhere to be seen when that happened! My later misspent youth was engaged in the delights of Sniggery Woods, birds' egg and butterfly collecting, and perhaps being chased by the local bull in a nearby field!

'MH'

Carol singing and ice-cream cake

Wow, what memories the photographs of Blundellsands brought back to me when I saw them on the Frith website. I lived in Sudbury Road and have such happy memories of Crosby Beach which is where I spent my childhood, also of the Brighton Le Sands community and especially the mums, we never dared do much wrong in those days as there was always someone to tell our mums!

Another memory I have of my young days in the area is of carol singing around the houses at Christmas time and then going to buy ice-cream cake with the proceeds afterwards, however one time we made the mistake of carol singing at St Nicholas's Church Vicarage and Mr Nye (the vicar) made us give all our proceeds to charity, so there was no ice-cream cake that evening!

Joyce Brown

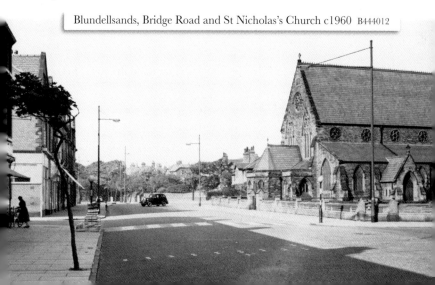

Blundellsands, Bridge Road and St Nicholas's Church c1960 B444012

A little book of memories

The Fairground and Tower at New Brighton

New Brighton, The Pier c1960   N14039

I remember well the 'Tower' at New Brighton in the 1960s, as well as the fairground at the resort, with all the rides that did their best to make you sick after the hotdogs and the candyfloss. Who got a kiss in the ghost train, or at least a cuddle from their girlfriend? Everywhere there was the smell of food and the constant sound of music playing so loud.   *Peter Buttress*

An Eiffel-style Tower at New Brighton opened in 1898, which at 631ft high was the tallest structure in England at the time. The tower also included the Tower Buildings at its base, and Tower Gardens. The whole complex was a focal point of entertainment, including a theatre, ballrooms, roller and ice-skating rinks, a menagerie and a boating lake. Sadly, the tower became unsafe and was dismantled between 1919 and 1921, but the Tower Buildings at its base (which included the famous Tower Ballroom) continued to attract the crowds until 1969, when the structure was destroyed by fire.

New Brighton, The Tower and the Sands 1900   45163

New Brighton, The Beach c1960   N14025

The nutcracker

The ride in the middle of this photograph of the children's playground on the beach at Southport was known as a 'copper's helmet', and the nearest one on the left was called 'the nut cracker'. As the nutcracker swung higher and higher the children standing on the ends had to watch out that they didn't crack their heads ('nuts') on the cross members.

Julia Skinner

Southport, Peter Pan's Playground c1955 S160043

Childhood fun at Pensby, near Heswall

When I was young in the 1960s we lived first on Fishers Lane in Pensby, then moved to Barleyfield Road where my little sister was born in the front bedroom of number 1. We walked down to the junior school on Greenbank Drive every day, three little kids holding hands through fields of barley that towered over our heads! Then the builders came. Before we knew it

> "I was petrified of walking through Old Wood Road because of the vicious dog that lived there and nearly always ran after me!"

we were walking home through little streets like Bennett Walk. The houses went up so fast that I got lost walking home one day! At the bottom of Barleyfield Road they built an old people's home which meant we could not get through to Fishers Lane any more, we had to go round through Old Wood Road instead. I was petrified of walking through Old Wood Road because of the vicious dog that lived there and nearly always ran after me! Weekends for us children were spent playing up at 'Devils Dyke' where the boys had made a rope swing. We 'nicked' potatoes from our kitchens, lit a fire and tried to bake them, they were rock-hard but we ate them anyway! We also walked miles through fields and farms up to Thurstaston Common in complete safety, fearing only the bulls! On the way back we would pray that our dad would be in the Irby Club in Irby, where we would stop off in the hope of scrounging some much needed refreshment off him.   *Debbie Ranson*

Happy days at 'Hoylake Baths'

I recall many happy memories of the Hoylake bathing pool from when I was young. 'The baths' used to attract large attendances in those days. The pool had two fountains spurting over fake rocks. We used to climb on these to cool off. In those days the summers seemed to go on forever. I remember that when the baths were closed on warm evenings, me and a crowd of friends would climb over the rear walls to enjoy free swimming until the police came and we all had to scarper. It was all great fun and full of laughs, life was so much better in those days.   *Ron McShane*

My mum used to take us down to the Hoylake Baths when I was young in the 1960s, some friends would come too and she usually ended up with eight of us. We'd all pile on to the bus at Irby, with the picnic basket and sundries. We had great fun on our outings to Hoylake.   *Alan Sharp*

Hoylake, The Swimming Pool c1965 H277010

Soaking in the hot water at Guinea Gap Baths!

I was born and brought up in Bridle Road at Seacombe, near Wallasey, in 1944. I remember the Guinea Gap Baths well from my childhood, but my memories of the baths are not of going swimming in the pool, but to have a bath; I think they had about four baths. It was heaven to soak in a real bath with hot running water, instead of the old tin bath that was brought out once a week at home! Happy memories!

Marge Olney

Why I didn't bother going to see The Beatles...

My family spent many holidays in the Wallasey-New Brighton area in the 1960s. We'd get the 'Royal Iris' ferry boat across the Mersey to Liverpool to look around the shops, go swimming at Guinea Gap Baths and also go to the New Brighton Pool to watch the 'Miss New Brighton' beauty contests. I remember on one of our walks along the front to New Brighton we saw an advertisement introducing a new group called The Beatles – I remember thinking they couldn't even spell their name right, so I wouldn't bother going to see them…if only! How I wish I could turn back the clock...

Sue Meek

1960s Tunnel Memories

I clearly remember the Land Rover 'Tunnel Patrol' police vehicles seen in this photograph of the Queensway Tunnel. I was always puzzled by their cream colour as ordinary police vehicles were either all white or sky-blue with white doors. My family visited my grandmother in Tranmere virtually every week, and my dad used to play a game on the way home with me and my mother when it was dark, called 'How Many Cars in the Tunnel Without Lights?'. We had to guess how many cars would be seen in the tunnel without any lights on, and whoever guessed the closest to the actual total won the game. You were supposed to leave your vehicle's lights on in the tunnel, but many people turned them off as its interior was quite brightly lit. I had three cousins who used to collect the Mersey Tunnel tickets. They were in various colours (a kind of pink, a blue and a light green) and they had a broad central stripe with a different coloured edge. Quite why they collected them, I never knew!   *Brian Jones*

Birkenhead, Queensway Tunnel c1965 B399027

The good old days – childhood pranks in Birkenhead

When I was a kid in the 1950s we lived in the Abbey Buildings at Birkenhead, at the side of the building to the right of the Queensway Tunnel in the photograph on the opposite page. The tunnel area was a play area for us kids, and we would also play on the gardens at the front of the tunnel, as well as the nearby railway sidings – it was so different in them days. We used to watch bikers on Sunday coming through the tunnel and from Woodside heading for Wales, hundreds of cyclists all whistling as they went past. There weren't many cars in them days, as such. As kids we also used to go down to Woodside, pay to go on the ferry if we had the money to do it, and then hide in the toilets, go back and to all day till we got found out and got kicked off, then go and get our name stamped on the piece of aluminium on the machine. Then we'd go and play on the floating bridge at the side of Woodside and on the buses parked up till the ticket man gave us a kick up the backside. The good old days.

"The good old days."

Bill Devaney

Memories of Birkenhead market

I have many memories of the market at Birkenhead when we were kids. I remember lining up at the end of the day at the indoor café in the market (I think it was called Olivaries) for the leftover crusts off the loaves of bread, spread with Stork (or Echo?) marge. All the kids got there for 5 o'clock for the free butties. Plus I remember the Jewish guy Eli in the corner, everyone would go there at Christmas for the kids' pressies. He would sell anything, he was there till it was closed down. I also remember the guy who sold ointments and powders for all skin problems, and the women who sold secondhand books at the back of the market by the steps. The new market is not a patch on the old one, good times were had in the old market.

Bill Devaney

When the first supermarket opened at Woodchurch, Birkenhead

I remember the first supermarket opening in Woodchurch, it was in New Hey Road, I don't know the exact year but it was about 1958. I went to the opening with my mum and they had a competition to guess the weight of a chicken. My mum guessed the correct weight and she won a pan!

Pamela Hignett

When I was a child in the 1950s...

I lived in the Garston district of Liverpool as a child in the 1950s, and I can clearly remember pushing my doll's pram up to these shops with my mother from our home nearby in South Mossley Hill Road. I was always fascinated by the overhead cash delivery system in the Co-op shops, although we did not frequent the Co-op food shop very often, with my father being a shopkeeper himself – buying groceries from there was strictly forbidden. The very end shop was the Co-op selling haberdashery and shoes, I think that was where my love for shoes was born, and a cake shop called Waller's was next door, another favourite place of mine. Happy days!

Margaret Ralph

Liverpool, Holmefield Road from Booker Avenue (Garston) c1955 L60018

Bonfire Night in Berwick Street

I grew up in the 1950s in Berwick Street, Liverpool. The best night
of the year was Bonfire Night. My mates and I would collect bonny
wood for ages before the big night and store it in a bombed out
house on Berwick Street. The whole street would contribute
stuff to burn. On November 5th we'd run home from school and
get the wood out and place it at the junction of Berwick Street
and Proctor Street ready for our dads to light it. I can't remember
there ever being any trouble. What I do remember is everyone in
the street having a wonderful time.

David Clarke

We built the Biggest Bonfire!

This memory is about Bonfire Night at Blundellsands in 1953. I was
thirteen at the time and lived off Riverslea Road, which led down
to a walled field on to the beach. My friends Derek Austin, Les Reece,
Charlie Kelly, Ray Betts and a few others had built the Biggest Bonfire
for miles around. We had travelled as far as Formby to collect all
sorts of wood, old gates and so on. Three of us stayed overnight
to protect it from other kids pilfering the wood for their bonfire,
feeding off lemonade and roast potatoes until the day the fire was
to be lit – November 5th. Then it rained nearly all that day, and we
all wondered if we would be able to light the bonny that evening.
Ray Bett's dad was chief mechanic at the garage at the top of
Warrenhouse Road on Bridge Road, we went to see him and he gave
us all the old oil from the sumps of the oil changes he had done to
use as fuel. Then the bonfire started all right, and it stayed alight for
nearly three days, with plenty of roast potatoes cooked on it after all
the fireworks had finished. HAPPY DAYS!

Thomas Davies

Our picnic at Billinge Lump

I was brought up in St Helens and Billinge was a hilly country village that was five miles away. In the summer of 1949 or 1950 a group of us children of all ages took sandwiches and bottles of pop or water for a picnic on Billinge Lump. The official name for it is Billinge Hill, but anyone who has lived locally always refers to it as the Lump. The Lump is the highest ground in the area from which you can see both the Liverpool Cathedrals and also, on a really clear day, the reflection on the River Mersey.

On the top of the Lump is a small square stone building, somewhat neglected, and this point is one of the signal points around the country that would have had a bonfire beacon lit on it to signal the approach of an invading army/armada etc. On the sunny day we went for our picnic there, the hill

> "It was a great adventure, with no adults to limit our play and no thought given to any danger."

(then covered in ferns) and the surrounding woods provided a great place for playing hide and seek and generally having a good time. Having eaten all our sandwiches, we used the paper bags to collect blackberries. We ate lots of them, grubs and all, then carried the rest home in soggy paper bags for our mums to make into bramble jam.

It was a great adventure, with no adults to limit our play and no thought given to any danger. It is still such a happy memory to me, and I wonder how many of the group who went with me on that day still remember it?

Sylvia Kendrick

My Bootle, 1971 to 1976

I was born and brought up in Bootle, at number 27 Monfa Road, next to the junction of Aughton Road. I have great memories of Bootle at that time. Mrs Gallagher's shop at the bottom of Aughton next to Orrell Primary School was a treat, what a lovely little woman she was. Then there was Cousins the bakers, where my grandad used to get my cottage pies for my lunch, which I came back from school for, and Brady's the newsagent, where I bought my grandad's Woodbines from. Then there was St John and St James Church, the little dairy shop and the launderette ('the baggy') a little further on past Willard Street. I have great memories of 'John the Modelcraft' at the top on Harris Drive, that was the treasure trove of all toy shops, any kind of model tank, aeroplane, or boxes of soldiers could be bought there. It was a special place in those days, the Klondyke area, now (2013) in the process of being demolished and redeveloped, never to be the same again. RIP the Bootle I knew and loved.   *Ian Breeze*

The way it was – Orrell Park in the 1950s

I remember as a little girl running to the sweet and tobacconist's shop on the corner of Westfield Road in the Orrell Park district of Liverpool, where we lived, for five Woodbines for my mum. The shop was owned by Tom Lewis. Obviously it wasn't a problem selling cigarettes to little girls then! As rationing was still on I would also be sent next door to Wormwell's, the grocer's shop, for 2oz of sugar – this was sold in a cornet of blue paper, which my mum called a 'screw of sugar'.
Carol Hughes

Toxteth remembered

I was born in Toxteth in 1946 and lived in Lamport Street (just off Warwick Street) until I was about 6 years of age, then because of town planning we had to move to Hawkstone Street. I wonder how many other people can share my memories of Toxteth at that time? Does anyone remember the fair that was on the Hollow (pronounced Olla) in Mill Street opposite Warwick Gardens?

> "Does anyone remember the fair that was on the Hollow?"

And what about the bakery on Mill Street that had the ovens right next to the pavement in the cellar, even in the winter you could sit on the pavement because of the heat from the ovens, ahh, I can still smell those hot barm cakes even now. We had some great shops in those days. On the corner of Park Road and Warwick Street was Milton's pawnbroker's shop, Whitaker's cake shop and café, and Yaffie's. Further down on Park Place was Capaldi's Milk Bar and Fredrick's Building Supplies next to St Patrick's School. And who remembers Costigan's on Mill Street? They had the same cable pulley system for payments that the Co-op shops had. After you'd made your purchase the shop assistant would put the cash in a container and then attach it to the pulley system and pull the wooden handle that would send the container shooting across the shop on wires to the cashier. Then your change would be returned the same way.

Richard Green

Marsh's pie shop at Haydock –
'the best pork pies in the world'

When I was young and living in Haydock in the 1960s, a favourite place of mine was Marsh's pork pie shop in Old Whint Road. Their pork pies were known as the best in the world and we kids at Jagger's (Richard Evans Junior School, West End Road) used to sing "Marsh's, they make the best meat pies" to the tune of 'Colonel Bogey'. I can't remember the other words. The pies were baked in a commercial oven at the back of the shop and there was always a queue waiting when the oven doors were opened and the tray of hot pies was brought into the shop to be sold. The jelly on the top of the pastry was hot and liquid so you had to be careful carrying one home. There was always a cat sitting in the shop window, next to the cakes (the pies never got into the window, they sold immediately). The cat put my mum off buying anything there but it didn't bother me! You could also buy sweets there, my favourite being Holland toffee, banana flavour. Those were the days!

Ann Atherton

The place to go was Sherrie's Milk Bar...

I grew up in Ellerslie Road, in the Tuebrook area of Liverpool. When I was young, the most exciting place for the local teenagers to go to was Sherrie's Milk Bar on the corner of Dorset Road in Tuebrook, where you could sit in the warm, buy a soft drink for 'coppers' and listen to the new technology – the 'Juke Box'.

Pam Williamson (née Craig)

Sliced bread! Whatever next!

The shop with the white awning in the row on the right of this photograph of Myers Road East in Crosby was Scott's Bakery, which surprised us with sliced bread (!!!) in the 1950s. On the extreme edge on the right foreground of this view is the side of Jump's Dairy – their cows would come in through that gap between the front and the other shops further down. In the 1940s and early 1950s, the grocer's on the corner on the left hand side used to sell butter from a great lump; the request for "A pound of butter please" would have the gent carving off about that amount and 'patting' it with butter pats into a manageable shape before weighing and wrapping it in greaseproof paper.

John Kelly

Crosby, Myers Road East c1960   C357009

The toy stall at Earlestown market

I loved the Friday markets at Earlestown when I was young in the 1960s. The crowded stalls transformed the drab market square, which was filled with the cries of the stall-holders and the bustle of shoppers, their baskets laden with fruit and veg.

My favourite stall was the toy stall and I spent all of my weekly pocket money here. I used to buy fake cigarettes with their puff of 'smoke', and fake flies that looked so incredibly real to an 8-year-old – I used to hide them in a slice of bread or cup of tea to scare my mum and grandma. As fascinating as all the toys were, for me the biggest

> "At market end I would trundle home with orange boxes for firewood kindling all tied together with string."

draw to this stall was the store-holder who always wore a scarf and fingerless gloves and had a perpetual drip on the end of his nose – I would delay my purchase for as long as I could, waiting and waiting to see if that tremulous drip would finally drop! At market end I would trundle home with orange boxes for firewood kindling all tied together with string, and stuffed with discarded lettuce leaves for our rabbits, dragging the lot noisily down Haydock Street. If I was really lucky my mum would treat me to hot raisin toast spread with thick melted butter in the café across from the bus stops.

Sharon High

My memories of Earlestown as a youth in the 1960s

I remember Earlestown market in the 1960s, there used to be rabbits hung up on a stall there and I used to feel sorry for them. We always had black puddings off the market – it was years later that I found out what they are made of, and now I wouldn't eat one if I was starving. Haircutting was always done by Mr Hacket on the market square, he was always smoking and ash used to drop on the gown covering your clothes.

The shops in Earlestown used to be run by the same people for years, Anikin's fruit shop in Market Street, Mort's groceries, Arthur Smith's ironmongers in Market Street, Peak's chemist in Queen Street, Lyon's fish shop in Bridge Street. There used to be a Mr Goulding who came round with household goods, he had a 'house shop' in Earlestown but I can't remember which street it was in. His mother used to run the shop with him.

I also remember the chip van which used to park near Davies Avenue, their chips always seemed to taste better if they were eaten outside. They were all wrapped in newspaper then, there was no plain paper first as there is nowadays.

George Woodward

Every Sunday!

Every Sunday for years during the summer holidays this is where you would find me, my mam, dad, three brothers, two sisters, aunties, uncles, cousins, nanny and grandad. We would park the car what seemed like miles away and then trek over the sand dunes to the 'beach' – I use the term loosely, as when we used to go there in the 1960s we'd have to dodge oil slicks, broken glass, burnt mattress springs and then the jelly fish before we could paddle in the murky waters! Who knows what pollution there was in those days, we just took it for granted that this was what a beach looked like. Years on, we would think back to all that with horror. The sand dunes were great though, we used to spend hours jumping off them!

Susan Miney

Formby, The Beach c1960 F106019

Drivers of a certain age

This is a nostalgic picture for drivers of a certain age. The two round 'No Waiting' road signs seen on either side of the road in this photograph of Formby are a reminder of when and where you could park your car when you went shopping in the past. These signs were used during the 'unilateral waiting' period in the 1950s, when vehicles could wait on one side of the road on odd days of the month and on the opposite side on even days. The signs were hinged in half moons so that they could be tipped over to show which side of the road was currently available for parking.

Julia Skinner

Formby, The Post Office and the Village c1955 F106003

Good times at Thurstaston

As a youngster in the 1960s I lived at Thurstaston, on the west side of the Wirral Peninsula overlooking the Dee estuary. I sang in the choir at St Bartholomew's Church for a short time, which was an awe-inspiring place. I spent some time down on the Dee, walking out to the middle at low tide, and playing in the old gun garrison overlooking the Dee until someone yelled "Ghost!" and we ran away like startled hares. I particularly liked to sit on top of the cutting looking out over fields and the Dee to Wales, it was so peaceful you could hear a curlew call down below. But best of all was sledging on Sutton Hill and the common until you were so cold you would cry.

Alan Sharp

Thurstaston, The View of the Welsh Hills c1950 T174006

The Shrimp Boats at Heswall

As a young kid in the 1950s I used to walk down Banks Road at
Heswall with my mother to the slipway and buy fresh shrimps
from the Evans boys. The shrimps were caught in the Dee and
cooked on board the boats on the way back to the slip. The fishing
was a thriving industry in those days.   *Pete Buttress*

Shrimps and barley sugar at Heswall

My nanny and gampi lived on Banks Road at Heswall in the 1960s.
My nanny (Tilly Wilson) used to shell the locally-caught shrimps in
her kitchen – I've never seen anyone move as fast as her when she
was doing it. My sister and I used to visit our grandparents on our
way down to Heswall shore and the shrimps would be piled high in
the middle of the cold stone floor. On the way back from the shore
we always stopped at the sweet shop at the top of Banks Road and
bought a barley sugar stick for 2d, if it wasn't for that I don't think I'd
have managed the long walk home to Pensby.   *Debbie Ranson*

Heswall, The Slipway c1955   H276063

My schooldays at Heswall

I have many memories of walking up School Hill at Heswall as a child when the road was covered in sheet ice – which was made even more slippery by us 'skaters'. At the top of the hill in my day was a sweet shop run by a Mrs Sharpe, which was a treasure trove for us youngsters. I was a pupil at the primary school at the top of School Hill from 1954 until passing the 11 plus in 1959 and going to Calday Grammar School. The headmaster was 'Pop' Edwards who had been there for donkey's years – he was there when my dad was a pupil at the school!

We pupils used old-fashioned nib pens and the best job in the world was to be ink monitor. This involved mixing

Heswall, School Hill c1955 H276047

powdered ink with water in a large metal jug on a Friday morning and then going around every classroom to fill up the inkwells on the desks. I don't think our mums were too happy when we returned home more blue than white after being on ink monitor duty!

Much of the school had been damaged when Heswall was bombed in May 1941, during the war, and for all the years I was there no repairs were done and there were huge mounds of rubble where once there were classrooms. These areas were strictly off limits. Today's Health & Safety bods would have heart attacks if they saw where we learnt and played in those days! The kitchens had also been destroyed and food for our lunch was brought to school from (I think) the Puddydale Council School kitchens. I remember the food was always lukewarm, but it was very tasty otherwise. There was no hot water, the school had outside toilets and old coke-fuelled heating which smelled wonderful but wasn't very effective at warming such an old damaged building, yet we all survived. My classroom for my final year was 'the prefab' which was stuck on the playing fields next to the main school and was the only modern building on the site.

I loved my time at Heswall school, and it was very traumatic moving from this small, caring, friendly place of about 300 children to Calday Grammar with 900 boys, which was run as if it were a public school and very impersonal.

It was only a lifetime ago!

Peter Bufton

I went to Our Lady's School at Formby...

I attended Our Lady's School at Formby in the 1960s, which used to be in Church Road (demolished 1986). My most abiding memories of those times are of the nuns who ran the school and were very strict, and also how antiquated it was. The school still had gas lights which were lit on dark winter afternoons and emitted an eerie green glow, the refectory had long wooden tables and benches, and the outside loos were something to behold! We used to be taken to benediction once a week at the church, which was next door, and had to sing in Latin. The kids these days don't know how easy they have it!

Mal Jones

Formby, Chapel Lane 1957   F106005

'Ellergreen versus St Tessies'

I went to Ellergreen School in the Norris Green district of Liverpool in the mid 1950s, and well remember having stone-chucking and snowball fights with the kids of 'St Tessies' (St Teresa's School), who used to call us 'College Puddings'. I remember there was a great chippie on the corner of Carr Lane at Norris Green where we schoolkids used to go at lunchtime and stuff the chips into half a 'Vienna' loaf.

> "I well remember having stone-chucking and snowball fights with the kids of 'St Tessies'."

DEE-licious...! That was much better than the school nosh. I often got the cane for it – but those chips were worth it!

John Jay

Coal in the school swimming pool

My first school was Harrington Board School in Toxteth, which was on the corner of Grafton Street and Stanhope Street. I started there in 1950. The main thing I remember about this school was that it had a tiny swimming pool in its basement, but the pool wasn't used for swimming, they used it to store coal for the school boiler!

Richard Green

My early career as a milk-boy

I have so many wonderful memories of Earlestown and Newton-le-Willows and surrounding areas when I was young. As a boy in the 1950s I used to deliver milk for Christie's dairy. Milk in those days was mainly delivered by horse-and-cart and the round I was on covered all of Newton and the Wargrave area, from memory I think Bill Christie had four or five horse-and-cart runs and one van run. On some Sunday mornings two of us used to finish our runs by the Old Crow Inn on Crow Lane East and we would race the horses back to the farm which was next to the Oak Tree Hotel on the corner at the end of the lane – this was only done when the full time milkman didn't turn up for work though, and the boy assistants were left in charge. What other memories of those times could be told, just the thought of them brings a wonderful grin to my face, so many tales, eh boys?!

Ralph Waldie

Newton-le-Willows, The Oak Tree Hotel c1960 N149023

On point duty

This photograph of Southport shows a member of the local constabulary on point duty in Lord Street in the mid 1950s. The wearing of white coats was introduced in some towns during the Second World War, and gave policemen at least a sporting chance of not being run down by traffic during the blackout. There was even a plan in the 1960s to issue policemen on point duty

> "A white coat gave policemen at least a sporting chance of not being run down by traffic."

with helmets that had a revolving light on top! Strange how that idea never caught on…!   *Julia Skinner*

Southport, Lord Street c1955 S160038

Royal Liverpool Children's Hospital

The children's hospital at Heswall was a branch of the Royal Liverpool Children's Hospital in Myrtle Street, Liverpool. The Heswall hospital was opened in the early years of the 20th century on a 9-acre site bordering Telegraph Road, opposite the large grass area near the centre of town known as the 'Puddydale'. The hospital originally had a series of open-air wards with verandahs to the rear of the building, with one side of each ward being totally open to the elements. The philosophy at the time was that fresh air would help clear congested lungs, particularly with diseases such as TB. The wards were later enclosed when opinions about the nation's health changed. The Heswall hospital closed in 1985 and was demolished in 1989; a Tesco supermarket now occupies the site.

Heswall, The Royal Liverpool Children's Hospital c1965   H276144

Merseyside

My stay at the Royal Liverpool Children's Hospital at Heswall

I was in the Royal Liverpool Children's Hospital at Heswall a number of times in the late 1940s, suffering from bronchiectasis, a lung disease. I always went into Hugh Owen Thomas Ward. It was a long ward separated by sliding doors, with the girls at one end and the boys at the other. I remember sleeping out on the verandah every night unless it was raining or foggy! On fine days the nurses would pull our beds out onto the lawn. Every other night we would have to sleep over the 'Nelson', the boys one night and the girls the other. It was a wooden contraption that fitted over the bed frame, and we would sleep over it with our bottoms in the air! It was to aid postural drainage for patients with chest problems. The views from the ward were amazing. There were rolling lawns around the hospital going down to woodland, and one could see right over to the Welsh hills. Visiting was only allowed once a month, which to a child of 6 or 7 years old was an eternity. As I came from Liverpool it was a long trek for my mum and dad to get there to see me, they didn't have a car at that time so it was a bus, then a train, then another bus – it used to take them all day! As this was just after the war, sweets were still subject to rationing, but my uncle owned a sweet shop and used to send a goody bag for me with my parents. It was the rule for all sweets given to the patients to be taken from them and put in a sweet tin, then everyone in the ward would get a sweet after our evening meal – but my dad used to hide some in my pillowcase!

Maureen Alcock (née Woods)

Growing up in Kirkdale

I was one year old in 1956, when my family moved from Huyton with Roby to number 82 Brasenose Road in the Kirkdale district of Liverpool, so all my childhood memories are about growing up in Kirkdale. We had nothing but we were happy. There were six of us, we all slept in one bed, top and tail, but everyone in our road was the same. We never had a bathroom, just an outside toilet that looked like a shrine because we had that many candles in there. Every Saturday night all the mams and dads went out and would come home either fighting or singing. There was one feller who was about 60 and dead skinny and every Saturday night he would come home from the alehouse singing, and everyone called him 'the singing skull'. Every lamp post in our road was bent because we kids were always swinging on them. We had an old pram and two times a week we went for a quarter of coal to Charlie Clark's in St John's Road, that's when we could afford it, we had no doors or floorboards upstairs but we were warm. I was 15 when we moved out. The houses got knocked down, what a waste of a good community.

Patricia Johnson

> "There were six of us, we all slept in one bed, top and tail, but everyone in our road was the same."

The Coronation street party at Prescot, Sunday School 'treats' in Knowsley Park, and watching the Queen go past...

I remember going to a street party in Beaconsfield Street, Prescot, I think it must have been for Queen Elizabeth II's Coronation in 1953. I was about 4 at the time, and I remember sitting at a long table outside my grandma's house which was two doors up from Prescot C of E school. From approximately 1955 to 1959, I also remember going to Knowsley Park at Prescot each year for the Sunday School 'treats', which happened when we had completed the Whit Walks, when we walked round the town in procession behind our banners, wearing our best clothes. The procession ended in Knowsley Park (before it was a Safari Park), where we would have a party tea in a big marquee – sandwiches, cakes, jelly and cups of tea in white cups and saucers. After tea we ran races – for example the egg and spoon race.

Another memory from my childhood is when the Queen came to Prescot and we children waited to see her go past, standing opposite the council offices. We all had little flags. We waited for a long time, then her car was spotted in the distance. We raised our flags and – whoosh! She had gone past before we had time to wave them! I remember being very disappointed.

Audrey Edwards (née Lamb)

Romance on the number 77 bus

It was so interesting to see this photograph from 1964 on the Frith website, of the old number 77 bus at Woodside Ferry at Birkenhead. My husband-to-be in the 1960s worked on the Birkenhead Transport and I met him on the number 77 bus route going through from Woodside to Upton. We married in 1963 and are still together all these years down the road. Fond memories!

Brenda Vanderwert

Like Brenda Vanderwert (above memory), I also met my husband on the number 77 bus. Seems it was a magic number for meeting future husbands! We had many wonderful trips on this bus. After going to the pictures at night, we used to eat hot dogs upstairs in the front seat – there was a place at Woodside that made the best hot dogs. Thanks for the great memories, number 77!

Susan Hibbert

Birkenhead, The Ferry and Bus Terminus 1964 B399032

Learning to row a boat at Raby Mere

One Sunday in 1958 on a day out from New Brighton with my
family, playing French cricket on the field above Raby Mere, I
watched the rowing boats on the water. It looked such fun that
I went for a ride back to Raby Mere on my bike a few days later. I
wanted a row on one of the boats. The gentleman in charge said
it was a shilling (5p in modern money), but I could not afford
that. He told me to come back on a Saturday morning and I
could row all I wanted to for sixpence (the equivalent now of 2½
p), so I did. The kind man showed me the basics of rowing and
off I went. I dropped many an oar and caught many a crab but
after a few weeks I got the hang of it. Needless to say the water
took over my life and later on I joined the Royal Navy. I couldn't
row their boats though – too big!

David Lawton

Bromborough, Raby Mere c1955 B445306

The clock on the Royal Liver Building

When I was young, the giant clock on the Royal Liver Building at Liverpool was the only way to know the time of day (we had no watches then!).

You could see the clock when you were coming in from the New Brighton ferry, and work out what tram you would be on! In those days the tram-car home left the pier-head by this clock and got us home for tea – costing 1d (1 'old' penny) for a return fare.

John Williams

> "The giant clock on the Royal Liver building was the only way to know the time of day."

Liverpool, The Ferry Boats c1965 L60021

Liverpool, The Royal Liver Building c1955   L60019

FRANCIS FRITH

PIONEER   VICTORIAN   PHOTOGRAPHER

Francis Frith, founder of the world-famous photographic archive, was a complex and multi-talented man. A devout Quaker and a highly successful Victorian businessman, he was philosophical by nature and pioneering in outlook. By 1855 he had already established a wholesale grocery business in Liverpool, and sold it for the astonishing sum of £200,000, which is the equivalent today of over £15,000,000. Now in his thirties, and captivated by the new science of photography, Frith set out on a series of pioneering journeys up the Nile and to the Near East.

INTRIGUE AND EXPLORATION

He was the first photographer to venture beyond the sixth cataract of the Nile. Africa was still the mysterious 'Dark Continent', and Stanley and Livingstone's historic meeting was a decade into the future. The conditions for picture taking confound belief. He laboured for hours in his wicker dark-room in the sweltering heat of the desert, while the volatile chemicals fizzed dangerously in their trays. Back in London he exhibited his photographs and was 'rapturously cheered' by members of the Royal Society. His reputation as a photographer was made overnight.

VENTURE OF A LIFE-TIME

By the 1870s the railways had threaded their way across the country, and Bank Holidays and half-day Saturdays had been made obligatory by Act of Parliament. All of a sudden the working man and his family were able to enjoy days out, take holidays, and see a little more of the world.

With typical business acumen, Francis Frith foresaw that these new tourists would enjoy having souvenirs to commemorate their days out. For the next thirty years he travelled the country by train and by pony and trap, producing fine photographs of seaside resorts and beauty spots that were keenly bought by millions of Victorians. These prints were painstakingly pasted into family albums and pored over during the dark nights of winter, rekindling precious memories of summer excursions. Frith's studio was soon supplying retail shops all over the country, and by 1890 F Frith & Co had become the greatest specialist photographic publishing company in the world, with over 2,000 sales outlets, and pioneered the picture postcard.

FRANCIS FRITH'S LEGACY

Francis Frith had died in 1898 at his villa in Cannes, his great project still growing. By 1970 the archive he created contained over a third of a million pictures showing 7,000 British towns and villages.

Frith's legacy to us today is of immense significance and value, for the magnificent archive of evocative photographs he created provides a unique record of change in the cities, towns and villages throughout Britain over a century and more. Frith and his fellow studio photographers revisited locations many times down the years to update their views, compiling for us an enthralling and colourful pageant of British life and character.

We are fortunate that Frith was dedicated to recording the minutiae of everyday life. For it is this sheer wealth of visual data, the painstaking chronicle of changes in dress, transport, street layouts, buildings, housing and landscape that captivates us so much today, offering us a powerful link with the past and with the lives of our ancestors.

Computers have now made it possible for Frith's many thousands of images to be accessed almost instantly. The archive offers every one of us an opportunity to examine the places where we and our families have lived and worked down the years. Its images, depicting our shared past, are now bringing pleasure and enlightenment to millions around the world a century and more after his death.

For further information visit: www.francisfrith.com

INTERIOR DECORATION

Frith's photographs can be seen framed and as giant wall murals in thousands of pubs, restaurants, hotels, banks, retail stores and other public buildings throughout Britain. These provide interesting and attractive décor, generating strong local interest and acting as a powerful reminder of gentler days in our increasingly busy and frenetic world.

FRITH PRODUCTS

All Frith photographs are available as prints and posters in a variety of different sizes and styles. In the UK we also offer a range of other gift and stationery products illustrated with Frith photographs, although many of these are not available for delivery outside the UK – see our web site for more information on the products available for delivery in your country.

THE INTERNET

Over 100,000 photographs of Britain can be viewed and purchased on the Frith web site. The web site also includes memories and reminiscences contributed by our customers, who have personal knowledge of localities and of the people and properties depicted in Frith photographs. If you wish to learn more about a specific town or village you may find these reminiscences fascinating to browse. Why not add your own comments if you think they would be of interest to others? See **www.francisfrith.com**

PLEASE HELP US BRING FRITH'S PHOTOGRAPHS TO LIFE

Our authors do their best to recount the history of the places they write about. They give insights into how particular towns and villages developed, they describe the architecture of streets and buildings, and they discuss the lives of famous people who lived there. But however knowledgeable our authors are, the story they tell is necessarily incomplete.

Frith's photographs are so much more than plain historical documents. They are living proofs of the flow of human life down the generations. They show real people at real moments in history; and each of those people is the son or daughter of someone, the brother or sister, aunt or uncle, grandfather or grandmother of someone else. All of them lived, worked and played in the streets depicted in Frith's photographs.

We would be grateful if you would give us your insights into the places shown in our photographs: the streets and buildings, the shops, businesses and industries. Post your memories of life in those streets on the Frith website: what it was like growing up there, who ran the local shop and what shopping was like years ago; if your workplace is shown tell us about your working day and what the building is used for now. Read other visitors' memories and reconnect with your shared local history and heritage. With your help more and more Frith photographs can be brought to life, and vital memories preserved for posterity, and for the benefit of historians in the future.

Wherever possible, we will try to include some of your comments in future editions of our books. Moreover, if you spot errors in dates, titles or other facts, please let us know, because our archive records are not always completely accurate—they rely on 140 years of human endeavour and hand-compiled records. You can email us using the contact form on the website.

Thank you!

For further information, trade, or author enquiries
please contact us at the address below:

**The Francis Frith Collection, 6 Oakley Business Park,
Wylye Road, Dinton, Wiltshire SP3 5EU.**

Tel: +44 (0)1722 716 376 Fax: +44 (0)1722 716 881
e-mail: sales@francisfrith.co.uk **www.francisfrith.com**